A majolica teapot by George Jones in naturalistic style with a monkey handle, c.1875. (Dreweatt Neate)

British Teapots and Coffee Pots

Steven Goss

A Shire book

Published in 2005 by Shire Publications Ltd,
Cromwell House, Church Street, Princes Risborough,
Buckinghamshire HP27 9AA, UK.
(Website: www.shirebooks.co.uk)

Copyright © 2005 by Steven Goss.
First published 2005.
Shire Album 446. ISBN-10: 0 7478 0634 9;
ISBN-13: 978 0 7478 0634 9.
Steven Goss is hereby identified as the author of this work
in accordance with Section 77 of the Copyright, Designs
and Patents Act 1988.

British Library Cataloguing in Publication Data:
Goss, Steven
British teapots and coffee pots. – (Shire album; 446)
1. Teapots – Great Britain – History
2. Coffeepots – Great Britain – History
I. Title 738.8
ISBN-10: 0 7478 0634 9.
ISBN-13: 978 0 7478 0634 9.

Cover: *An interesting and rare 'Marqueterie' fluted teapot by Doulton & Rix with exquisite decoration and an unusual pierced handle, c.1890. (Author's collection)*

ACKNOWLEDGEMENTS
The author would like to thank the following for their generous help with the illustrations
for this book: Francesca Vanke Altman and Ruth Fleming of Norfolk Museums Service
(Norwich Castle Museum); Mark Law (Law Fine Art); Clive Stewart-Lockhart and Liz
Peck of Dreweatt Neate Auctioneers, Newbury; John Axford of Woolley & Wallis
Auctioneers, Salisbury; Linzi Goss of Lawrences Auctioneers, Crewkerne; Nic Saintey of
Bearnes Auctioneers, Exeter; Adam Schoon of Tennants Auctioneers, Leyburn; Pam
Woolliscroft of Spode Museum Trust; Lyon & Turnbull Auctioneers, Edinburgh; Finan &
Co; Goss & Crested China Club; Special Auction Services; Dave Reed; Andrew Grant Fine
Art; John Fowkes; Marion Bond; John Manley; Jackie Brindley-Thomas; and other private
collectors who wish to remain anonymous.

Printed in Malta by Gutenberg Press Limited, Gudja Road, Tarxien PLA 19, Malta

Contents

Early wares 4

New styles of the nineteenth century 18

The Edwardian and Art Deco periods 30

Other collectable teapots 35

What to look for 40

Further reading 46

Places to visit 47

Index 48

Staffordshire salt-glazed stoneware teapot, boldly decorated with a rose on a deep red ground, c.1750. (Woolley & Wallis)

Early wares

When the ships of the East India Company began regular sailings to China in the mid seventeenth century it took more than a year for a cargo of tea to reach England. Traders promoted the strange new drink as having extraordinary medicinal qualities, capable of curing headaches, fevers, scurvy and other ailments. The leaves were considered a valuable commodity that had travelled from distant exotic lands, and tea was so expensive that only the very wealthy could afford to drink it.

The high status of tea was further enhanced by the curious equipment needed to prepare it. The attractive and delicate porcelain spouted pots and handleless cups (now known as teabowls) brought with shipments of tea were much admired, and tea-drinking soon became a status symbol. English potters did not know the secret of making porcelain and their coarse earthenware vessels could not easily withstand boiling water, so the imported Chinese porcelain wares were essential.

Coffee reached England in about 1637 and coffee-houses became popular meeting places to drink and socialise. These establishments were for men only and provided an ideal setting to discuss politics and other important matters. Chocolate was also a favourite beverage in

A coffee-house in the late seventeenth century. These establishments were for men only and sold alcohol as well as tea, coffee and chocolate. (Private collection)

An early octagonal coffee pot with straight tapering sides, wooden side handle, domed cover with volute thumb-piece, and a spout formed as a bird. London, 1719. (Dreweatt Neate)

the seventeenth century for those who could afford it, and the fashionable coffee-houses of London sold ale, wine and brandy in addition to tea, coffee and chocolate.

By the beginning of the eighteenth century, tea, coffee and chocolate each had their own distinctive vessels for serving purposes. The earliest silver teapots were pear-shaped and often panelled for added strength. They were also small – reflecting the high price of tea. The government levied high taxes on tea, supposedly to protect the coffee industry, and a pound of tea cost as much as a week's wages for a skilled craftsman.

After 1720 the bullet-shape teapot became fashionable. This simple rounded shape was usually undecorated, but the polished surface was ideal for engraving the original owner's crest or armorial if required. At first, bullet teapots had plain straight spouts, but by 1730 curved and fluted spouts had become popular as one fashionable shape evolved into the next.

Coffee pots and chocolate pots are both tall and slender so that the spout is kept above the sediment. The main difference between them is that the latter has a hinged or detachable cap in the lid through which a *molinillo* (or *molinet*) was fitted, rather like a plunger, to stir

An early bullet-shape teapot with a fruitwood handle and a typical short straight spout of the period. Hallmarked for 1721. (Dreweatt Neate)

up the chocolate sediment into a frothy drink. Tapering cylindrical chocolate and coffee pots with high domed covers and side handles were the norm until about 1730, although chocolate pots are quite rare.

Tea was brewed in a teapot by adding boiling water to infuse the leaves, whereas coffee pots were used only as serving vessels. The coffee would be brewed in a large kettle over a fire and then transferred to the coffee pot for serving at table. The pot would then be kept warm on a stove. Some silversmiths made special matching stands incorporating a lamp or burner on which the pot could rest to keep the contents warm.

One of the problems that had to be overcome was preventing heat from the boiling water in the metal pot being transmitted to the handle. A metal handle would be impractical, so handles were generally made of wood. Later, during the nineteenth century, there was a fashion for silver teapots to have silver handles, but with bone or ivory insulators to protect the pourer.

Ceramic teapots did not have this problem and manufacturing techniques had improved by the 1730s. Primitive-looking slipware pots were superseded by white salt-glazed stoneware, which had the considerable advantages of being lightweight and easily moulded.

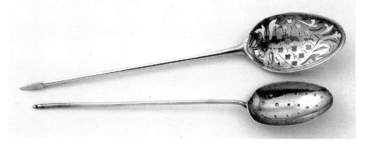

Early eighteenth-century silver mote spoons. The pierced bowl was used for skimming tea-leaves, and the spiked handled was for unclogging the teapot spout. (Woolley & Wallis)

These wares were fired at a very high temperature, which partly vitrified the body, and when the kiln was at maximum heat salt was thrown into it. The salt vaporised and sealed the body with a thin clear glaze that did not obscure any moulded detail.

Two major advances in the 1740s transformed ceramic manufacturing. The first of these was the development of cream-coloured earthenware. This creamware was lead-glazed and more durable than the tin-glazed earthenwares commonly known as delftware. It was created by adding calcined flint, which improved the ware's resistance to thermal shock, making it ideal for tea and coffee pots.

The second important development was the emergence of porcelain production in England. A formula for making a type of soft-paste porcelain had been discovered and English manufacturers began to

Agateware teapots, c.1750. The decoration is formed from different coloured clays. Birds and animals were popular subjects to use as finials. (Norwich Castle Museum)

A Staffordshire redware teapot and two examples of moulded salt-glazed stoneware teapots. All c.1750. (Norwich Castle Museum)

produce items in imitation of Chinese porcelain imports.

Teapots and coffee pots, together with matching teabowls and coffee cups, were among the first items made. They were painted by hand and usually bore an oriental-inspired design similar to the imported examples they were copying. Factories at Chelsea, Bow and Vauxhall in London and others at Worcester, Derby and Liverpool were soon successfully manufacturing porcelain tea and coffee pots to cater for an increasing demand.

Two early globular teapots with very different styles of decoration. One is painted in enamel colours with a portrait (possibly Bonnie Prince Charlie), c.1755, and the other has naturalistic leaves and tendrils applied on to a brown glazed body, c.1750. (Norwich Castle Museum)

The style of ceramic teapots broadly followed the style of their silver counterparts, so early porcelain and creamware teapots are generally small and rounded, copying the bullet design in silver, and are referred to as being of globular shape.

Silver teapots dating between 1750 and 1770 are surprisingly scarce, perhaps because of the enthusiasm with which English porcelain was received by the wealthier social classes. In the 1750s the

Silver teapot, inverted baluster shape, with cast decorated spout and engraved coat of arms. London, 1758. (Woolley & Wallis)

Three porcelain coffee pots: (left) Worcester, with Chinese-inspired polychrome decoration; (centre) Derby, with a simple floral design in enamel colours; (right) Worcester, painted in underglaze blue with the 'Mansfield' pattern; all c.1760–70. (Norwich Castle Museum)

latest fashion for silver teapots was the inverted baluster shape. This top-heavy style was not particularly successful and was more commonly found in Scottish silver. It was largely ignored by porcelain manufacturers of the time.

Coffee pots took on a baluster shape for much of the later eighteenth century, generally conforming to practicality rather than innovative design, but teapots were appearing in novel forms. By the 1760s they were being made in the shapes and colours of cauliflowers, pineapples and animals, demonstrating that novelty teapots are not a new idea. Pineapples were rare and exotic fruits and a symbol of hospitality. Eighteenth-century houses sometimes had pineapple finials on their gateposts as a way of welcoming guests, so the fruit was particularly suitable as a design for something as socially important as a teapot.

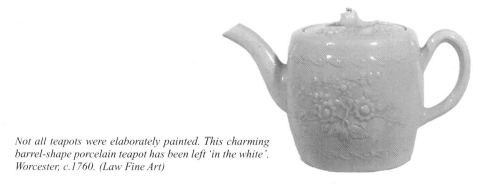

Not all teapots were elaborately painted. This charming barrel-shape porcelain teapot has been left 'in the white'. Worcester, c.1760. (Law Fine Art)

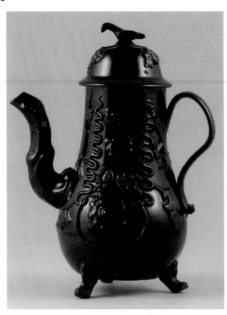

A Jackfield coffee pot with strap handle and scroll-moulded spout. Jackfield is a generic name for a class of earthenware decorated with a glossy black glaze that was traditionally made at Jackfield in Shropshire. (Woolley & Wallis)

Below: *Staffordshire creamware teapot moulded as a cauliflower, c.1765. (Woolley & Wallis)*

(Left) Tapering cylindrical silver coffee pot engraved with the owner's crest. The finial is in the form of a pineapple. London, 1746, by Peter Archambo. (Right) Silver teapot, oval shape with bright-cut decoration. London, 1785, by John Robins. (Linzi Goss)

A typical porcelain coffee pot of about 1765. This one was made at the factory of Richard Chaffers in Liverpool and painted in 'famille rose' style. (Woolley & Wallis)

Another advance at this time was the invention of Sheffield plate by Thomas Boulsover. This substitute for silver was made by fusing a sheet of silver to an ingot of copper in a furnace. The resulting material could then be rolled or hammered to make decorative and useful objects such as teapots.

In the third quarter of the eighteenth century silversmiths made teapots and coffee pots from sheet silver. The drum-shape teapot, which first appeared in about 1770, was well suited to this type of manufacture. Teapots in this shape are usually simple in outline, relying on bright-cut engraving to enhance their appearance. Silversmiths also re-introduced angles and corners to teapot shapes, probably to compete with the makers of fused plate,

(Left) Staffordshire salt-glazed coffee pot moulded with overlapping scallop shells and an animal spout, c.1755. (Right) Wedgwood creamware, transfer-printed with the Tea Party pattern, c.1770. (Norwich Castle Museum)

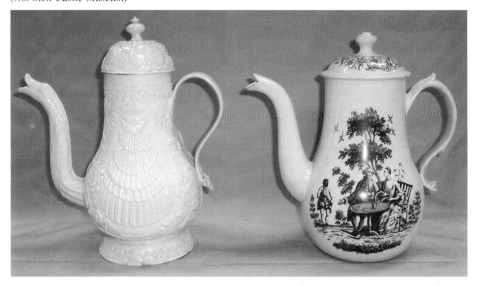

who would have had difficulty concealing tell-tale traces of copper in such a design.

Neo-classical styles, popularised by architects such as Robert Adam, were also fashionable. The Greeks and Romans did not have teapots, but that did not deter manufacturers from inventing modern classical ones. Teapots made of basalt, a black vitreous stoneware created by Josiah Wedgwood, are often found decorated with classical subjects.

Wedgwood is also associated with several other ceramic innovations used in the manufacture of tea and coffee pots. One of these is pearlware, which was developed from creamware by using a cobalt-tinted glaze to make it appear whiter and more like porcelain. Another is jasper, a fine unglazed stoneware that is usually blue, though other colours occur. A third is caneware, a buff stoneware thought to have

A standard-size Lowestoft porcelain teapot and five miniature teapots. The lid of the miniature Worcester teapot on the right is not the original as it is slightly too big and painted with a non-matching pattern. These blue and white examples all date from c.1755–80. (Norwich Castle Museum)

*A finely moulded teapot
such as this would
usually be painted by
hand. Transfer prints
were not easy to apply
to moulded wares, and
the painter could use his
skill to emphasise the
raised design. Made by
Philip Christian & Co,
Liverpool, c.1770. (Law
Fine Art)*

the colour of bamboo, which it often simulates. Teapots made with a
bamboo appearance are very striking. It should be noted that although
Wedgwood is credited with the development of these materials many
other manufacturers also produced goods made from them.

One further dry-bodied medium that was very popular with
manufacturers of tea and coffee pots is redware. Like basalt, it was
particularly well suited for relief-moulded neo-classical designs.

The blue and white decoration commonly found on eighteenth-
century teapots was either painted or transfer-printed on to the body
before it was glazed. The substance used was metallic oxide of cobalt,
which was black when applied and turned blue only after firing, so the
painter had to use his skill and experience to judge how the tones and
shading would look on the finished article. Transfer-printing, using an
etched copper plate, allowed manufacturers to produce a large number
of identical pieces at relatively low cost. The technique was introduced
in the 1750s but did not become widespread until after 1770.

High taxes on tea meant that smuggling was widespread, and even
clergymen could be tempted to overlook the law. In 1777 Parson
Woodforde of Weston Longville in Norfolk records that 'Andrews the
smuggler brought me this night about 11 o'clock a bag of hyson tea …
He frightened us a little by whistling under the parlour window just as
we were going to bed.'

Ale had been the staple British drink for centuries, but a series of
poor grain harvests had made it too expensive for many people and in

Creamware coffee pot with a moulded mask spout and beautifully painted in enamel colours, c.1770. (Lawrences)

1784 the government was persuaded to reduce the tax on tea. As soon as tea was more affordable, people began to drink it in larger numbers and the demand for teapots and other tea-related items grew.

British potters were given a further boost in 1791 when the directors of the East India Company decided to abandon the porcelain trade and the vast shipments of Chinese porcelain ceased. This momentous decision left a void in the market, especially as Britain was involved in a war in Europe at that time and no European porcelains were being imported either. The result was an unprecedented expansion of the pottery industry.

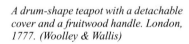

A drum-shape teapot with a detachable cover and a fruitwood handle. London, 1777. (Woolley & Wallis)

Scottish silver teapot, urn shape. The hallmarks are incomplete, but the pot was made in Edinburgh, c.1780. (Woolley & Wallis)

Above: *(Top left) An unusual creamware teapot, possibly Leeds. (Top right) Pearlware shell-moulded teapot with replacement lid. (Front) Leeds creamware by William Greatbatch with religious motto. All c.1780–90. (Norwich Castle Museum)*

Teapots celebrating notable people: (top) Reverend John Wesley, transfer-printed in black, c.1790; (bottom) Frederick the Great of Prussia on a salt-glazed stoneware teapot, c.1760. (Norwich Castle Museum)

Creamware teapot, drum-shape with strapwork handle. Painted with harvest scenes and the motto 'God speed the plough', c.1790. (Andrew Grant)

The vertical fluting and wavy oval outline of this silver teapot with matching stand mirrors contemporary ceramic teapots of the 1790s. James Mince, London, 1792. (Woolley & Wallis)

Six porcelain teapots, probably all from the New Hall factory in Staffordshire, copying the silver shape that was fashionable in about 1800. New Hall was one of the first factories to introduce pattern numbers, and each of these designs has a different pattern number painted on the base. (Woolley & Wallis)

(Rear) Leeds pearlware with spaniel finial, c.1800. (Front left) Pearlware pointed oval shape, c.1800. (Front right) Creamware with armorial crest and lady finial, c.1790. (Norwich Castle Museum)

Teapots were now larger and oval shapes were the new fashion. Many ceramic examples were still painted by hand, but transfer prints were being increasingly used to cut the cost of production and this further opened the market to the less wealthy. By the end of the eighteenth century tea had replaced ale at the breakfast table and established itself as a popular drink among all sections of society.

New styles of the nineteenth century

During the first years of the nineteenth century there were important advances in the manufacture of porcelain. After much experimentation, potters developed a type of hard-paste porcelain that was particularly fine, and by 1815 the process had been perfected. The recipe included calcined animal bones, which strengthened and whitened the body and enabled items to be made with a thinner gauge. The new 'bone china' was also more reliable in the firing process, resulting in fewer losses. These were significant improvements and bone china is still the standard British porcelain body made today.

The increased popularity of tea-drinking was mirrored by a rapid increase in the number of porcelain manufacturers. There were twenty-seven factories in Britain in the 1780s, but this had grown to one hundred and six in production during the decade 1810–20.

Competition was fierce, and manufacturers blatantly copied a successful shape or new design produced by their rivals. As a result, many teapot shapes were popular for only a few years before being superseded by the latest fashionable design, so knowing when a style was in vogue can be a useful aid to dating.

The *old oval* shape was the basic teapot form during the period 1790 to 1810. The shape was widely employed by silversmiths and workers in silver plate, and quickly copied by ceramic manufacturers. A touch of individuality could be added by varying the shape of the handle or

Coalport oval teapot and stand. The spiral fluting indicates a date of 1800–5. (Law Fine Art)

A Castleford-type white stoneware example showing the sliding lid design found on this style of teapot; c.1810. (Law Fine Art)

spout, and it is these subtle differences that can help to identify exactly where a teapot was made.

A ceramic variation of the old oval shape has a wavy outline and is known as *commode* shape. It is also commonly called *silver* shape, but this is a misnomer because most ceramic shapes were copied from designs in silver. It was popular during the same 1790 to 1810 period.

Another variation is the *low oval* shape, which is distinctive because it usually has a flared area of rim known as a 'cape'. Most teapots in this elegant style date from 1805 to 1815, the height of the Regency period. The profile is sleek and graceful, and it is easy to see how designers adapted the basic oval shape to develop each successive variation on the theme, including the *octagonal* shape, which was introduced in about 1800 and lasted for about a decade.

By 1810 the oval shapes were giving way to oblong forms, although one of the most popular new oblong shapes is rather confusingly

New Hall porcelain with cape rim, new oval shape, c.1810. (Law Fine Art)

London shape. This example is by Chamberlain's, Worcester, c.1820. (Law Fine Art)

Spode pearlware, low oval shape of about 1820. (Law Fine Art)

called *new oval*. It was given this name by the Spode factory and usually accompanied the graceful rounded cups of the period that are referred to as being 'Bute' shape. It is clearly a development of the old oval form, but is fatter, with a lid that often has a simple pointed knop and sits within a raised parapet.

Another important oblong shape is the *London*, which is associated with the distinctive 'London' shape cups introduced in about 1812. This was a very popular design and, in common with the other shapes mentioned, it was made in a wide range of ceramic materials. Most London shape teapots date between 1812 and 1825.

Silver lustre and copper lustre earthenware teapots made to imitate the metals. Both c.1815. (Norwich Castle Museum)

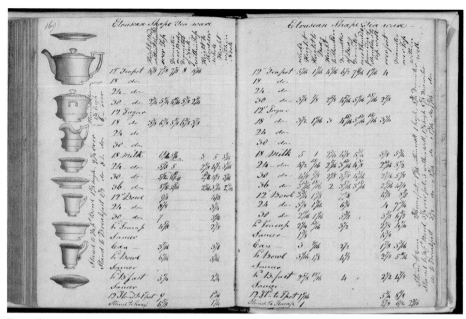

Pages from a workman's book at Spode Museum showing the precise dimensions of Etruscan-shape teawares, c.1820. The teapot measurements are given across the top row. (Spode Museum Trust)

Dating teapots is relatively easy, but identifying the manufacturer may not be so straightforward. Rival factories blatantly copied each other and many factories did not mark their wares, especially during the eighteenth century. The idea of numbering different patterns may seem an obvious practice for a large manufactory to undertake but it was not introduced until the 1780s, and even during the nineteenth century there were firms producing a substantial output of wares without a pattern numbering system.

The pattern number would be painted on to the underside of the teapot and can be helpful when

New oval shape decorated in Imari style with rich gilding. Spode's pattern number 967 is painted on the base, c.1815. (Law Fine Art)

Wedgwood red stoneware teapot decorated with Egyptian emblems, c.1820. The knop is formed as a crocodile. (Woolley & Wallis)

(Left) A Welsh variant of the London shape by Baker, Bevans & Irwin of Swansea. It is transfer-printed in green, c.1825. (Right) Worcester neo-rococo shape with petalled feet, c.1835. (Norwich Castle Museum)

Spode Felspar teapot and matching stand, c.1823. This octagonal shape was in production a few years earlier, but the desirable Felspar body was not introduced until 1821. An example of Regency quality. (Linzi Goss)

A political teapot bearing portraits of Lord John Russell and Baron Brougham and Vaux. It was made to commemorate the Reform Bill of 1832, which doubled the British electorate. (Dreweatt Neate)

Silver coffee pot of melon-fluted shape with ornate feet and flower finial, by William Hunter, London, 1837. (Woolley & Wallis)

trying to determine which factory was responsible for a particular piece. It was common practice to mark only certain items in a tea service, usually the larger pieces, but it is important to note that not every number found on the underside of a teapot is a pattern number. Some are tally marks applied by the decorator to identify his work. Many decorators were paid only for the pieces they painted, so they would add a mark to each finished item.

By 1825 the influence of the rococo was gathering pace. Teapots were becoming rounder, often raised on feet or pedestals, and the 1830s became a period of wild extravagance with elaborately moulded bodies painted with bold enamel colours and richly gilded. The rococo shape was ideal for such flamboyant decoration because gilding could highlight the flowing lines and ornate moulding to great effect.

An unusual form known as a *Cadogan* teapot was made during the 1830s. This curious design, derived from Chinese wine vessels, has no

A Cadogan teapot by Copeland & Garrett, c.1840. (Lawrences)

An early Victorian miniature teapot with a bold design of applied flowers and leaves. Made at the Minton factory, c.1840. (Law Fine Art)

lid and is filled by means of a hole in the base. An internal tube runs from the filling hole to the top so that it can be turned the right way up without spilling. It appears to be a most impractical idea because of the difficulty of removing used tea-leaves and general cleaning, and there is a theory that these vessels were not intended to be used as teapots at all. They may have been filled with brewed tea for serving, perhaps for amusement, but were probably designed for hot water.

During the 1840s a new, less expensive method of plating silver was introduced. Electroplating creates a thin coating of pure silver over a base metal by electrolytic deposition, a process patented by the Elkington Company of Birmingham. Electroplated items are whiter in appearance and lack the softer glow of Sheffield plate. The base metal was initially copper, but nickel was also used, hence the term EPNS

(Left) Electroplated Britannia metal coffee pot with engraved decoration, c.1880. (Right) Heavily embossed Victorian plated coffee pot, c.1860. (Linzi Goss)

An unusual Victorian miniature cube-shaped teapot by Yapp & Woodward, Birmingham, 1852. (Woolley & Wallis)

(electroplated nickel silver). Teapots and coffee pots bearing the similar stamp EPBM are made of Britannia metal, an alloy of tin, copper, antimony and zinc. Electroplate quickly became the new fashion and very little Sheffield plate was exhibited at the Great Exhibition of 1851.

The social importance of tea-drinking inspired a wide range of equipment deemed necessary to enjoy the beverage, from caddies and spoons to tables and trays, and ensured that every item associated with the drink would be made to a suitably high standard.

A typical light-hearted majolica design made by Minton. Fashionable teapots of this quality found a ready market. Date mark for 1859. (Finan & Co)

Minton majolica teapot modelled as a monkey, c.1860. (Dreweatt Neate)

Naturalistic design from the Belleek porcelain factory in County Fermanagh, Northern Ireland, moulded with wheat, berries and leaves, c.1875. (Law Fine Art)

These items would be especially used during afternoon tea, which became popular during the 1840s. Georgian and Victorian society was much more restrictive than today's and it was extremely important to have good manners. There were few better places to display good manners than around the tea table, and afternoon tea was an ideal occasion for young men and women to meet in a slightly less formal atmosphere.

There was a lack of innovative development in teapot style between the

Royal Worcester teapot decorated in naturalistic style, c.1885. (Woolley & Wallis)

A double-spouted Measham commemorative teapot, impressed 'Long live our noble queen 1887'. These treacle-glaze teapots are commonly known as 'bargeware'. Note the finial shaped as a teapot. (Tennants)

Late Victorian oval teapot. Note the insulators to prevent heat from reaching the handle. London, 1893. (Woolley & Wallis)

years 1840 and 1870 and the overall quality was in decline, although some fine teapots were still being made. Novelty teapots returned to popularity in the latter half of the nineteenth century, when design began to be treated as a serious moral issue. The Staffordshire firms of Minton and George Jones were leaders in this field and made some very desirable teapots as part of their majolica range.

An Arts and Crafts copper and brass teapot designed by Christopher Dresser for Benham & Froud, c.1890. (Dreweatt Neate)

A rare Martinware grotesque bird teapot, dated 1896. The four Martin brothers had a pottery at Southall in Middlesex and are well known for their art pottery bird sculptures and vessels. (Norwich Castle Museum)

Royle's self-pouring teapot. This earthenware example was made by Doulton, c.1895. The design was also made in silver, plate and pewter. (Author's collection)

During the 1870s some factories began to design teapots in naturalistic styles influenced by the Aesthetic Movement. The philosophy of surrounding oneself with natural beauty resulted in stylish teawares decorated with coloured and moulded flowers, leaves and flowing tendrils. Fashionable late Victorians wanted decoration that had been done by an artist, not a machine, and there were calls for a return to traditional values and hand craftsmanship.

The late Victorian period was also one of invention, with several innovative ideas being

Detail from a Burgess & Leigh teapot commemorating the Golden Jubilee of Queen Victoria in 1887. (Jackie Brindley-Thomas)

A silver teaset modelled as quail, by T. Smith & Son, Glasgow, 1895. (Tennants)

Left: *Late Victorian porcelain-lined teapot patented by A. E. Furniss. (Author's collection)*

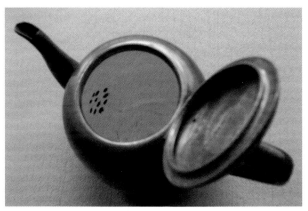

registered at the Patent Office. The most remarkable design is surely the invention of a self-pouring teapot, patented in 1886 by J. J. Royle. The metal cover has a deep flange, which is pulled up and then lowered while covering the vent hole with a finger, causing air pressure to dispense a cup of tea.

Another patent design is the porcelain-lined teapot registered by A. E. Furniss. It features a porcelain lining within a metal teapot and was probably intended to be a method of keeping the contents warm.

A very stylish Arts and Crafts plated teapot by Benson with a detachable tea strainer that clips to the peg at the top of the handle, c.1900. (Dreweatt Neate)

The Edwardian and Art Deco periods

At the turn of the twentieth century teapots were being made to commemorate all kinds of special events. Queen Victoria's Golden Jubilee in 1887, her Diamond Jubilee in 1897 and her death in 1901 were all marked by commemorative teapots, as were the coronations of King Edward VII in 1901 and King George V in 1911. These teapots were sold as souvenirs to record the occasion and are very collectable today.

Art Nouveau styles were also flourishing at this time, typified by the stylish pewter tea services sold by Liberty & Co as part of their 'Tudric' range. The range was introduced in 1902 and some of the designs are attributed to Archibald Knox, who created modern teapot shapes influenced by the ancient styles and motifs of Celtic art.

It was during the Edwardian era that a giant teapot, heralded as the largest in the world at that time, was made by Gibson & Sons of Burslem in Staffordshire. It stands 2 feet 6 inches (76 cm) high, weighs about a hundredweight (50 kg) and takes two

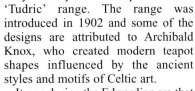

Typical Edwardian part-fluted three-piece teaset with matching hot-water jug, by Mappin & Webb, Sheffield, 1904. (Woolley & Wallis)

This Edwardian teaset by Hutton, London, 1903, is in its original lockable travelling case. (Woolley & Wallis)

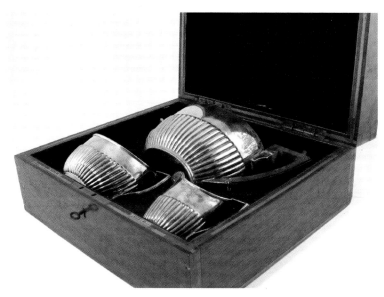

strong men to lift it when empty. The teapot was probably made as a promotional piece and is reputedly capable of holding 1024 cups of tea.

In contrast, some of the miniature teapots and coffee pots made by British potters are very small. A miniature teapot is usually no more than about 3½ inches high (9 cm), but an eighteenth-century miniature tea service known to the author contains a teapot that stands

The SYP ('simple yet perfect') teapot invented in 1905. Tea-leaves are put in the pierced upper section, water is added, and the pot is placed on its back to allow the tea to brew. When the tea is nearly ready the pot is tilted to 45 degrees and then placed upright so that the leaves and brewed tea remain separate. Perfect! (Marion Bond)

Silver six-piece tea and coffee service, fluted bombé shape, hallmarked for 1908. This set includes a tea caddy. (Law Fine Art)

only 2 inches (5 cm) high, including a rather prominent finial on the lid. Most miniature teasets were probably made as children's toys and not travellers' samples as is sometimes suggested.

The First World War significantly curtailed production and manufacturers were generally rather cautious in the years that followed, but some of the smaller factories were prepared to embrace the new fashionable styles of Art Deco and produce teapots that were more distinctive than those of their rivals.

One of these firms was Shelley. It marketed its designs to an increasingly fashion-conscious public by using the 'Shelley Girl', who appeared in newspaper and magazine advertisements, and by giving each teapot shape a trendy name such as Vogue, Eve or Regent.

Crested china became a popular souvenir for travellers when the expansion of the railway network enabled people to take day trips and holidays. This little teapot has a thistle finial and the crest of South Queensferry in Scotland. (Goss & Crested China Club)

(Left) Shelley 'Boo Boo' teapot designed by Mabel Lucie Attwell, c.1928. (Right) Clarice Cliff 'conical' shape teapot in the Umbrellas and Rain pattern, c.1929. (Linzi Goss)

Art Deco design is characterised by clean lines, geometric shapes and the use of motifs such as crescent moons, stars and polka-dots, and all of these features may be seen in the teapots of Susie Cooper, who worked as a designer and decorator for A. E. Gray & Co.

Susie Cooper trained at the School of Art in Stoke-on-Trent under the influential Gordon Forsyth and was inspired by his vision of new designs that endorsed simplicity of form and decoration. Most devotees of her work will admire the geometric and cubist designs in brilliant colours, but she was quite indifferent about them, often dismissing them as 'crude'. By 1933 her designs had changed considerably and she was producing teawares in simple but elegant styles made of earthenware and painted in pastel colours.

Art Deco styling with bold rectangular shape and angular handles. The tall vessel is a hot-water jug. Hallmarked for 1938. (Law Fine Art)

(Left) 'The Cube' teapot made by Foley: a practical design ideally suited for stacking on trays in hotels or teashops. This example dates from about 1940, but the design first appeared in the 1920s. (Right) Susie Cooper, 'Kestrel' shape, c.1930. (Norwich Castle Museum)

The name most associated with Art Deco ceramics is Clarice Cliff, whose daring designs in outrageous shapes and vibrant colours were both innovative and futuristic. She was influenced by contemporary artists such as Picasso and Mondrian and began work in a small studio at Wilkinson's Newport Pottery in 1927. Wilkinsons were quick to test the market with her ultra-modern ideas, and when the Bizarre range was offered to the public her employers were astonished that it sold so quickly. The Conical range, introduced in 1929, has the triangular handles that are the very essence of Art Deco ceramic design. Her teapot designs may be divided into three categories – landscape, geometric and floral – and each of the many patterns she created has a name.

Other factories producing interesting teapots of quality during the 1920s and 1930s include Burgess & Leigh (Burleigh), E. Brain & Co (Foley China Works), Wedgwood, Carlton and Royal Worcester. The onset of the Second World War brought an end to the Art Deco period and closed an era in which design and craftsmanship had flourished.

A 'War against Hitlerism' teapot, c.1939. These teapots were given to householders in exchange for aluminium saucepans needed to help the war effort. (John Manley)

Wade novelty teapot of a man wearing a flat cap. (Lyon & Turnbull)

Other collectable teapots

The function of a teapot does not set a tight limit on the shape it can take, which makes it the perfect object for a designer to demonstrate how weird, wonderful or wacky his or her imagination can be. Novelty teapots have been created in almost every conceivable guise and they form one of the collecting fields covered by this chapter.

The 1930s were good years for novelty teapots. Perhaps the best-known examples from this decade are the 'racing teapots' made in the form of racing cars by James Sadler & Sons of Stoke-on-Trent, who also made novelty teapots in the shape of aeroplanes and tanks. A teapot in the form of a crown was made to commemorate the

A Norwich City Football Club novelty teapot, and two 'racing teapots' designed as sports cars. (Norwich Castle Museum)

Wade Heath novelty teapot of Donald Duck. This design was made in three sizes. (Dave Reed collection)

coronation of King George VI in 1937, and other novelty designs include teapots modelled as cats and dogs with the head as the lid. Caricature figures and faces were another popular idea.

Teapot manufacturers have always been keen to promote new concepts and improvements, trying to gain an advantage in a competitive market. Some ideas focused on designs for a better, non-drip spout, such as the 'Perfecta' tea or coffee pot made by Booths, which featured the Camel patent dripless spout and was claimed to pour perfectly. Other designs concentrated on ways of keeping the tea hot by insulating the teapot with a removable chrome cover. These were sold under brand names such as Heatmaster, Everhot and Nevvacold.

The walking teapot made by Carlton Ware in the mid 1970s is a modern classic. It was designed by Danka Napiorkowska and Roger Michell and stands on little legs, complete with socks and shoes.

The Perfecta tea or coffee pot showing the patented dripless spout design. It was manufactured by Booths during the 1930s and marketed as being suitable for both tea and coffee. (Author's collection)

Walking Ware teapots were made in several sizes. Collectors also look for variations in the shoe and sock decoration. The cross-legged teapot was made as a limited edition and has the handwritten initials of designers Roger Michell and Danka Napiorkowska on the base of a shoe. (Dave Reed collection)

Today, potters are as enthusiastic as ever about putting their design ideas into practice and there are several small potteries that specialise in the manufacture of novelty teapots. Their wares are finding a ready market among collectors.

Studio pottery, the making of pots by hand in a small studio rather than a factory, has its roots in the opposition to mass-produced industrial ceramics. Early influential pioneers such as Bernard Moore and Michael Cardew objected to the standardisation of cheaply made crockery with little or no sense of who had made it.

Several of the most notable studio potters are linked by either having

Four novelty teapots, including a Portland Pottery foxhunting teapot, c.1950, and a Beswick panda eating bamboo, c.1990. (Private collection)

A Lowerdown Pottery coffee pot and stoneware teapot. Both pieces are marked with the seal of David Leach. (Woolley & Wallis)

worked together or by family ties. Cardew was Bernard Leach's first student. In 1926 he established the Winchcombe Pottery in Gloucestershire, which was subsequently bought in 1946 by his employee Ray Finch, who ran the business until 1979, then handing over to his son, Michael.

The Lowerdown Pottery at Bovey Tracey in Devon was set up by David Leach, son of Bernard. His stoneware tea and coffee pots are marked with his seal, and his later porcelain wares are characterised by fine carving and a celadon (pale green) glaze. His three sons, John, Jeremy and Simon, are all fine potters.

An earthenware teapot by the notable studio potter Alan Caiger-Smith, who worked at Aldermaston Pottery, near Newbury, Berkshire. It is date-coded for 1961. (Bearnes)

Troika Pottery teapot with bamboo handle, c.1970. (Woolley & Wallis)

Other prominent teapot-making potteries to look for are those at Hornsea, Rye, Aylesford, Poole, and the Troika Pottery in Cornwall. The Aldermaston Pottery in Berkshire is also noteworthy for the work of Alan Caiger-Smith. The salt-glazed teapots of Walter Keeler, with their sharply defined handles and spouts, are both expressive and intriguing.

In addition to those already mentioned, a few other key names to seek out are Jim Malone, Derek Emms, Geoffrey Whiting and John Solly, who all made interesting studio pottery teapots.

Ceramic artists continue to use the teapot as a theme for investigating ideas about art and craft, providing us with surprising objects that perform a commonplace job. In doing so, they have turned the much-loved teapot into an object of contemplation or display, while still allowing it to perform its original function as effectively as ever.

Two studio pottery teapots by Walter Keeler. The stoneware example on the left has brown and blue glazes and an impressed 'WK' seal mark, 1981. The mottled teapot was made in 1994. (Norwich Castle Museum)

What to look for

As a general rule, the value of an item is determined by factors such as its age, condition, rarity, level of craftsmanship, aesthetic quality and maker. For silver tea and coffee pots, other aspects such as the weight of the silver, the assay office and the clarity of the hallmarks may also be important considerations for a collector.

Look for tea and coffee pots made by notable silversmiths such as Philip Rollos, Ebenezer Coker, Paul Storr and Benjamin Smith, or by members of the Bateman family, especially Hester Bateman, a lady silversmith.

The lid of a silver pot should be part-marked. This is in addition to the main set of hallmarks found on the body of the item. If the lid has

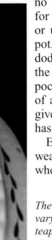

no marks, be suspicious. It is not unknown for a spout to have been added to a damaged or unfashionable tankard to create a coffee pot. Another favourite ploy of the 'duty dodger' was to submit a small disc of silver to the assay office, supposedly the back for a pocket watch, and then insert it into the base of a made-up coffee pot. This trick is often given away by solder marks where the disc has been added.

Examine the hinge on the lid for any weakness or restoration, and check the point where the handle joins the body to make sure

The tea strainer and number of straining holes can vary. Here we see nine holes in a Staffordshire teapot, and an innovative domed strainer in a similar example. Domed strainers are less likely to clog when pouring. Both c.1815. (Private collection)

The creamware coffee pot on the left was painted by hand. Note how freely the border design is painted compared to the transfer-printed Enoch Wood pearlware example. (Norwich Castle Museum)

it is secure. Check around the spout and the finial. Breathing on any suspect areas can help to reveal repairs.

Old Sheffield plate has become very collectable and can be worth as much as the equivalent silver piece. Most early examples are unmarked, although some makers used a symbol. Nineteenth-century Sheffield plate may have marks resembling the hallmarks found on sterling silver, and caution is necessary. If a piece is stamped 'Sheffield Plate', it is electroplate made in Sheffield during the twentieth century. Edges should be carefully examined for wear. A little copper showing through is generally considered to be acceptable, attractive even, but a larger amount is not.

Above: Bullet teapot with a cape rim and detachable cover. It is inscribed underneath: 'Bequeathed by Capt. Robert Dalrymple of the 3rd Regt of Guards who fell by a musket shot at Talavera de la Reyne on the 28th July 1809 to Capt. Chas. L White of the same Regt as a token of esteem and affection ...' The Battle of Talavera (in Spain) was part of the Peninsular War. Researching your purchases can be very rewarding. (Woolley & Wallis)

Left: At a glance this looks like a silver teapot, but this close relation is called an Argyll and is used for gravy. Opening the lid reveals an inner container for boiling water to keep the surrounding gravy warm. Hallmarked for York, 1790. (Woolley & Wallis)

Miniature pearlware teapot, c.1810. Note how the glaze has 'pooled' just above the footrim and is quite blue – a common feature of pearlware. (Law Fine Art)

Electroplated tea and coffee pots of the later nineteenth century are gaining popularity, especially those by an eminent maker such as Dixon & Sons, Elkington or Walker & Hall. They are relatively inexpensive and complete services are still easily found.

Ceramic tea and coffee pots were often treasured items. If they broke, they were not necessarily thrown away but lovingly repaired for further use. The fact that so many old teapots have survived is testament to how they have been kept and cherished through the years.

Spouts, handles and finials are particularly vulnerable to chipping and cracking and may have been broken off and re-attached. Faint hairline cracks are quite common and usually not too serious in an old teapot if the crack is short and stable. Lids are also vulnerable to damage and have sometimes been lost altogether. If the pot has a lid,

A Newlyn copper Arts and Crafts coffee pot with hammered decoration of stylised fish, c.1910. (Woolley & Wallis)

This plated tea and coffee set was designed by Christopher Dresser for Hukin & Heath of Birmingham, c.1880. Dresser was one of the first independent industrial designers, and one of the most influential. His designs were decades ahead of his time and made him a household name. (Dreweatt Neate)

check that it is the correct one. Does the pattern match, and is it a good fit?

Restoration work on ceramics is not always easy to spot, but if you are buying from a reputable dealer, any restoration will be declared. If buying at auction, ask the auctioneer for a condition report, which should highlight any problems. Damage or restoration should always be reflected in the price.

There have been so many good manufacturers of ceramic tea and coffee pots that it is difficult to select only a few for special mention. From the eighteenth century, the earthenwares and stonewares of

A Royal Winton 'solitaire' breakfast set for one person, c.1950. (Law Fine Art)

A very stylish silver-plated teaset from Mappin & Webb. This service was designed by Eric Clements, who was responsible for designing a range of household items for Mappin & Webb during the 1960s. (Law Fine Art)

Whieldon, Greatbatch and Wedgwood are all noteworthy. Look for the fine porcelains of Chelsea, Worcester, Derby, Spode, Davenport, Daniel, Coalport, Mason, Minton and Ridgway. The Art Deco designs of Clarice Cliff, Susie Cooper and Shelley are all keenly sought, and the twentieth-century studio ceramic teapots of Michael Cardew, Walter Keeler and the Leach family also have enthusiastic followers.

Teapots and coffee pots are an important part of British social history and it is calculated that two hundred million cups of tea are

Motto ware. Teapots with phrases written in a rural style were produced by potteries in the south-west of England, most notably the Watcombe Pottery near Torquay, Devon. (Lawrences)

Exile Pottery satirical teapot of Queen Elizabeth II, with a corgi spout. Made in 1981. (Special Auction Services)

drunk in Britain every day. With the widespread use of teabags and instant coffee granules, we no longer need pots for making or serving these drinks, but there can be no denying the pleasure of sitting down and having a leisurely pot of tea made in the traditional way.

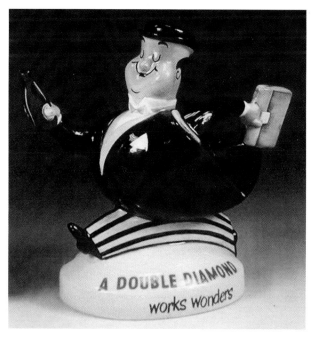

A humorous 1960s Beswick advertising teapot. (Private collection)

Further reading

Aguis, P. *China Teapots*. Lutterworth, 1982.
Atterbury, P. *Cube Teapot*. Antique Collectors' Club, 2000.
Berthoud, M., and Miller, P. *An Anthology of British Teapots*. Micawber, 1985.
Carter, T. *Teapots: The Collector's Guide*. Book Sales, 1998.
Clark, G. *The Eccentric Teapot*. Client Distribution, 1989.
Cushion, J. *Pottery and Porcelain Tablewares*. Studio Vista, 1976.
Emmerson, R. *British Teapots and Tea Drinking*. HMSO, 1992.
Ferrin, L. *Teapots Transformed*. F & W Publications, 2000.
Miller, P. *Teapots and Coffee Pots*. Midas, 1979.
Sandon, H. *Coffee Pots and Teapots*. Bartholomew, 1973.
Street-Porter, J. and T. *The British Teapot*. Angus & Robertson, 1981.
Tilley, F. *Teapots and Tea*. Ceramic Book Company, 1957.

A 'Tudric' pewter tea service and tray designed by Archibald Knox for Liberty & Co, of plain stylised form decorated with unpolished hammerwork and enamel cabochons, c.1905. (Dreweatt Neate)

Places to visit

The Allen Gallery, 10–12 Church Street, Alton, Hampshire GU34 2BW. Telephone: 01420 82802. Website: www.hants.gov.uk/museum/allen

Bramah Museum of Tea and Coffee, 40 Southwark Street, London SE1 1UN. Telephone: 020 7403 5650. Website: www.bramahmuseum.co.uk

Gladstone Pottery Museum, Uttoxeter Road, Longton, Stoke-on-Trent, Staffordshire ST3 1PQ. Telephone: 01782 311378. Website: www.stoke.gov.uk/museums

The Museum of Worcester Porcelain, Severn Street, Worcester WR1 2NE. Telephone: 01905 746000. Website: www.royal-worcester.co.uk

Norwich Castle Museum, Castle Meadow, Norwich, Norfolk NR1 3JU. Telephone: 01603 493625. Website: www.museums.norfolk.gov.uk

The Potteries Museum, Bethesda Street, Hanley, Stoke-on-Trent, Staffordshire ST1 3DW. Telephone: 01782 232323. Website: www.stoke.gov.uk/museums

Spode Museum and Visitor Centre, Church Street, Stoke-on-Trent, Staffordshire ST4 1BX. Telephone: 01782 744011. Website: www.spode.co.uk

Victoria and Albert Museum, Cromwell Road, South Kensington, London SW7 2RL. Telephone: 020 7942 2000. Website: www.vam.ac.uk

Wedgwood Museum and Visitor Centre, Barlaston, Stoke-on-Trent, Staffordshire ST12 9ES. Telephone: 01782 282818. Website: www.wedgwoodmuseum.org.uk

A potter making teapots at the Belleek porcelain factory in County Fermanagh in 1926. (Private collection)

Index

(Page numbers in italic refer to illustrations.)

Adam, Robert 12
Advertising teapot *45*
Aesthetic Movement 28
Agateware 7
Aldermaston Pottery 39
Archambo, Peter *10*
Argyll *41*
Art Nouveau 30
Arts and Crafts *27*, 30, *42*
Aylesford Pottery 39
Baker, Bevans & Irwin *22*
Bargeware *26*
Barrel shape *9*
Basalt 12, 13
Bateman, Hester 40
Belleek *26*, *47*
Benham & Froud *27*
Benson *32*
Beswick *37*, *45*
Bone china 18
Booths 36
Boulsover, Thomas 11
Bow 7
Britannia metal *24*, 25
Bullet shape *5*, 8, *41*
Burgess & Leigh 28, 34
Bute shape 20
Cadogan 23
Caiger-Smith, Alan *38*, 39
Caneware 12
Cardew, Michael 37, 38, 44
Carlton Ware 34, 36
Castleford *39*
Chaffers, Richard *11*
Chamberlains 20
Chelsea 7, 44
Chocolate 5, 6
Christian, Philip *13*
Clements, Eric *44*
Cliff, Clarice *33*, 34, 44
Coalport *18*, 44
Coffee-house *4*, 5
Coker, Ebenezer 40
Commode shape 19
Conical shape *33*, 34
Cooper, Susie 33, *34*, 44
Copeland & Garrett 23

Copper 11, 12, *27*, *42*
Copper lustre *20*
Creamware 6, 8, *10*, 11, 12, *14*, *15*, *16*, *17*, *41*
Crested china *32*
Cube shape *25*, *34*
Daniel 44
Davenport 44
Delftware 6
Derby 7, *9*, 44
Dixon & Sons 42
Doulton 28
Doulton & Rix *2*
Dresser, Christopher *27*, *43*
Drum shape 11, *14*, *16*
East India Company *4*, 14
Electroplate 24, 25, 42
Elkington 24, 42
Emms, Derek 39
Etruscan shape *21*
Exile Pottery *45*
Famille rose *11*
Finch, Ray 38
Fluted bombé shape *32*
Foley *34*
Forsyth, Gordon 33
Furniss, A. E. *29*
Gibson & Sons 30
Globular shape *8*
Gray & Co 33
Great Exhibition 25
Greatbatch, William *15*
Hornsea Pottery 39
Hukin & Heath *43*
Hunter, William 23
Hutton *31*
Imari style *21*
Inverted baluster shape *8*, *9*
Jackfield *10*
Jasper 12
Jones, George *1*, 27
Keeler, Walter 39, 44
Kestrel shape *34*
Knox, Archibald 30, *46*
Leach family 38, 44
Leeds *15*, *17*
Liberty & Co 30, *46*
Liverpool 7, *11*, *13*
London shape *20*, *22*

Low oval shape 19, *20*
Lowerdown Pottery *38*
Lowestoft *12*
Majolica *1*, *25*, 27
Malone, Jim 39
Mansfield pattern *9*
Mappin & Webb *30*, *44*
Marqueterie *2*
Martinware *27*
Mask spout *14*
Mason 44
Measham *26*
Melon-flute shape *23*
Mince, James *16*
Miniature teapot *12*, *24*, 31, 32, *42*
Minton *24*, 25, 27, 44
Moore, Bernard 37
Mote spoon 6
Motto ware *44*
Naturalistic style *1*, 8, *26*, 28
Neo-classical style 12, 13
Neo-rococo shape *22*, 23
New Hall *16*, *19*
New oval shape *19*, *21*
Newlyn *42*
Newport Pottery 34
Novelty teapot 9, 27, 35, 36, *37*, *45*
Octagonal shape *5*, 19, *22*
Old oval shape 18
Oval shape *19*, *20*, *21*, *27*
Pattern numbers *16*, 21
Pear shape 5
Pearlware 12, *15*, *17*, *20*, *41*, *42*
Perfecta 36
Pewter 30, *46*
Political teapot *22*
Poole Pottery 39
Porcelain 4, 6, 7, 8, 9, *11*, 14, *16*, 18
Portland Pottery *37*
Redware *7*, 13
Reform Bill *22*
Ridgway 44
Robins, John *10*

Rollos, Philip *40*
Royal Winton *43*
Royal Worcester *26*, 34
Royle, J. J. *28*, *29*
Rye Pottery 39
Sadler & Sons 35
Salt-glaze 6, *7*, *11*, *15*, 39
Scottish silver 9, *14*
Sheffield plate 11, *24*, 25, 41
Shelley 32, *33*, 44
Silver 5, 8, 9, *10*, 11, *14*, *16*, *23*, *29*, *32*, 40, *41*
Silver lustre *20*
Silver shape *16*, 19
Slipware 6
Smith, Benjamin 40
Smith, T. & Son *29*
Solly, John 39
Spode *20*, *21*, *22*, 44
Staffordshire *10*, *11*, *40*
Stoneware 12, *15*, *19*, *21*, 38, *39*
Storr, Paul 40
Straining holes *40*
SYP *31*
Tally marks 23
Transfer-printing *13*, *15*, 17, *41*
Troika Pottery 39
Tudric 30, *46*
Umbrellas and Rain pattern *33*
Urn shape *14*
Vauxhall 7
Wade 35, 36
Walker & Hall 42
Walking ware 36, *37*
Watcombe Pottery *44*
Wedgwood *11*, 12, *13*, *21*, 34, 44
Whieldon 44
Whiting, Geoffrey 39
Winchcombe Pottery 38
Wood, Enoch *41*
Worcester 7, *9*, *12*, *20*, *22*, 44
Yapp & Woodward *25*